MISSISSIPPI

The Magnolia State

BY
JOHN HAMILTON

Abdo & Daughters
An imprint of Abdo Publishing | abdopublishing.com

abdopublishing.com

Published by ABDO Publishing, a division of ABDO, PO Box 398166, Minneapolis, Minnesota 55439. Copyright © 2017 by Abdo Consulting Group, Inc. International copyrights reserved in all countries. No part of this book may be reproduced in any form without written permission from the publisher. ABDO & Daughters™ is a trademark and logo of ABDO Publishing.

Printed in the United States of America, North Mankato, Minnesota.
032016
092016

THIS BOOK CONTAINS
RECYCLED MATERIALS

Editor: Sue Hamilton   **Contributing Editor:** Bridget O'Brien
Graphic Design: Sue Hamilton
Cover Art Direction: Candice Keimig   **Cover Photo Selection:** Neil Klinepier
Cover Photo: iStock
Interior Images: AirPhoto, Alabama Dept of Archives & History, Alamy, Alfred Boisseau, American Cruise Lines, AP, Belzoni World Catfish Festival, Bill Stark, Biloxi Shuckers, Corbis, Dreamstime, Getty, Granger, Greene County, Gunter Kuchler, Hard Rock Hotel & Casino Biloxi, History in Full Color-Restoration/Colorization, iStock, Jimmy Emerson, Library of Congress, Minden, Mile High Maps, Mississippi Braves, Mississippi Brilla, Mississippi Dept of Archives and History, Mississippi RiverKings, NASA, National Geographic, New York Public Library, Ohio State Museum, Port of Pascagoula, Toyota Motor Manufacturing Mississippi, U.S. Army Center of Military History, U.S. Dept of Agriculture, Visit Mississippi, Wikimedia, and William Steene.

Statistics: *State and City Populations*, U.S. Census Bureau, July 1, 2015/2014 estimates; *Land and Water Area*, U.S. Census Bureau, 2010 Census, MAF/TIGER database; *State Temperature Extremes*, NOAA National Climatic Data Center; *Climatology and Average Annual Precipitation*, NOAA National Climatic Data Center, 1980-2015 statewide averages; *State Highest and Lowest Points*, NOAA National Geodetic Survey.

Websites: To learn more about the United States, visit booklinks.abdopublishing.com. These links are routinely monitored and updated to provide the most current information available.

Cataloging-in-Publication Data
Names: Hamilton, John, 1959- author.
Title: Mississippi / by John Hamilton.
Description: Minneapolis, MN : Abdo Publishing, [2017] | Series: The United
    States of America | Includes index.
Identifiers: LCCN 2015957617 | ISBN 9781680783261 (lib. bdg.) |
    ISBN 9781680774306 (ebook)
Subjects: LCSH: Mississippi--Juvenile literature.
Classification: DDC 976.2--dc23
LC record available at http://lccn.loc.gov/2015957617

CONTENTS

THE MAGNOLIA STATE

Mississippi is part of the Deep South region of the United States. It is named for the mighty Mississippi River, which meanders along most of the state's western border. Mississippi is a land filled with history, southern cooking, riverboats, and misty farm fields. In the countryside, the pace of life slows down on sweltering summer days, perfect weather for growing rows of corn, soybeans, and cotton.

In recent years, Mississippi has worked hard to find new opportunities. Today, the state's farms share the spotlight with growing cities. Busy factories produce everything from automobiles to aircraft parts.

Some of the most celebrated authors in history came from Mississippi. The state is also the home of the blues, the toe-tapping music that expresses so many hopes and dreams.

Mississippi is called "The Magnolia State" because of the many beautiful and fragrant magnolia trees that grow in its soil.

The *Queen of the Mississippi* riverboat cruises down the Mississippi River.

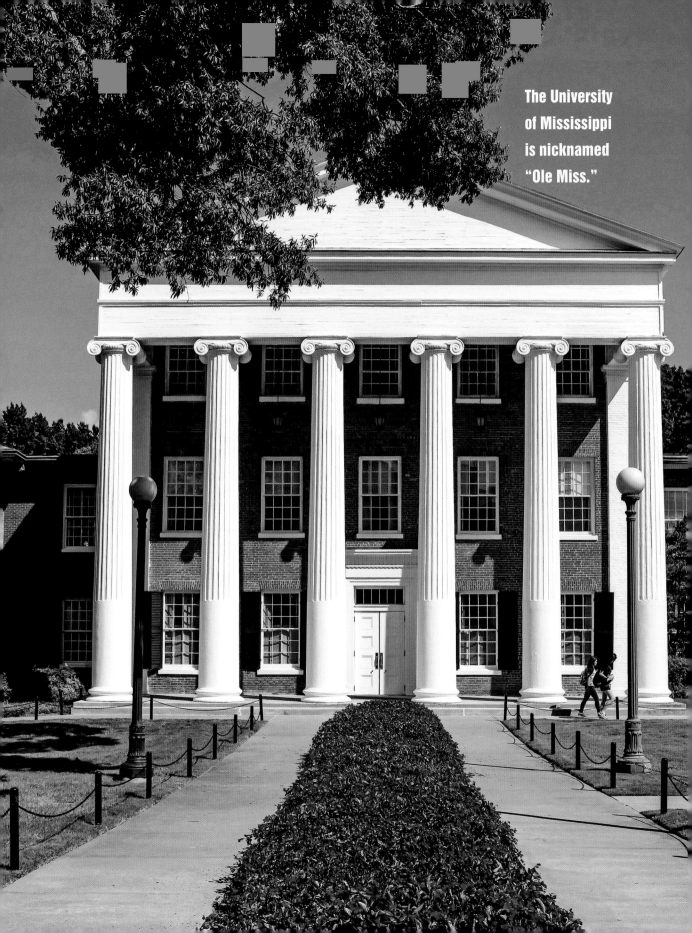

The University of Mississippi is nicknamed "Ole Miss."

QUICK FACTS

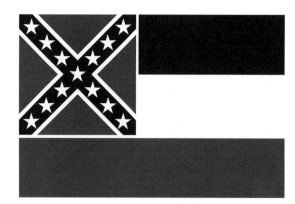

Name: Mississippi is named after the Mississippi River, which flows down the western border of the state. Mississippi is an Ojibwe Native American word that means "great river," or "father of waters."

State Capital: Jackson, population 171,155

Date of Statehood: December 10, 1817 (20th state)

Population: 2,992,333 (32nd-most populous state)

Area (Total Land and Water): 48,432 square miles (125,438 sq km), 32nd-largest state

Largest City: Jackson, population 171,155

Nickname: The Magnolia State, or The Hospitality State

Motto: *Virtute et armis* (By Valor and Arms)

State Bird: Mockingbird

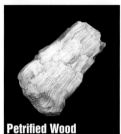

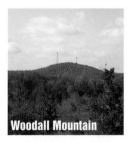

State Flower: Magnolia

State Rock: Petrified Wood

State Tree: Magnolia

State Song: "Go, Mississippi"

Highest Point: Woodall Mountain, 806 feet (246 m)

Lowest Point: Gulf of Mexico, 0 feet (0 m)

Average July High Temperature: 91°F (33°C)

Record High Temperature: 115°F (46°C), in Holly Springs on July 29, 1930

Average January Low Temperature: 34°F (1°C)

Record Low Temperature: -19°F (-28°C), in Corinth on January 30, 1966

Average Annual Precipitation: 58 inches (147 cm)

Number of U.S. Senators: 2

Number of U.S. Representatives: 4

U.S. Postal Service Abbreviation: MS

QUICK FACTS

GEOGRAPHY

Mississippi lies along the coast of the Gulf of Mexico in the southeastern United States. It is part of a region called the Deep South. The state's neighbor to the east is Alabama. To the north is Tennessee. To the south is the Gulf of Mexico and Louisiana. The Mississippi River winds its way down most of Mississippi's western border. Across the river to the west are Arkansas and more of Louisiana.

Mississippi's total land and water area is 48,432 square miles (125,438 sq km). That makes it the 32nd-largest state in the United States.

The land in Mississippi is mostly flat. Because the elevation is so low, there can be a lot of waterlogged areas during heavy rains.

Mississippi is mostly low and flat. Rain can cause areas to become waterlogged.

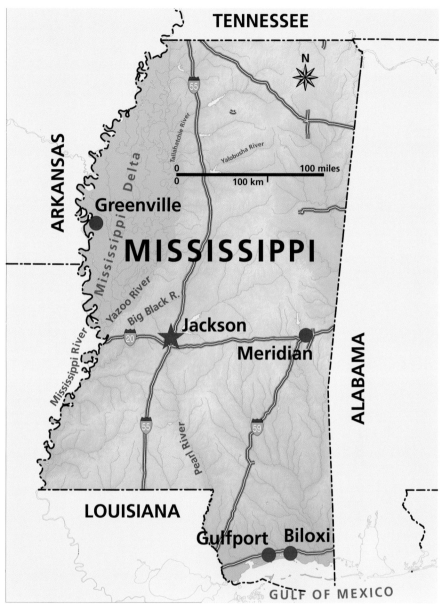

TENNESSEE

ARKANSAS

N

55

Tallahatchie River

Yalobusha River

0   100 miles

0   100 km

Delta

Greenville

MISSISSIPPI

Mississippi River

Yazoo River

Big Black R.

20

Jackson

Meridian

ALABAMA

55

Pearl River

59

LOUISIANA

Gulfport   Biloxi

GULF OF MEXICO

Mississippi's total land and water area is 48,432 square miles (125,438 sq km). It is the 32nd-largest state. The state capital is Jackson.

GEOGRAPHY

The state of Mississippi is divided between two main regions. The first is the Mississippi Delta region, also called the Mississippi Alluvial Plain. The Delta is in the northwestern part of the state. It fans out east from the Mississippi River, taking up about one-fifth of the state. Because of thousands of years of flooding by the Mississippi River, there is very rich clay soil in the Delta, suitable for raising crops such as cotton, soybeans, and rice.

The other four-fifths of Mississippi is called the East Gulf Coastal Plain. It starts at sea level at the marshy coast of the Gulf of Mexico. The land then slowly rises toward the north. The highest spot in Mississippi is in the very northeastern corner of the state. It is Woodall Mountain, which rises only to 806 feet (246 m). Like the Delta, the soil in the East Gulf Coastal Plain is very good for growing crops. There are also more woods and some gently rolling hills, including the Piney Woods in the south.

Piney Woods is southeast of Jackson, Mississippi.

A sandy beach near Gulfport, Mississippi. The coastline of Mississippi is less than 50 miles (80 km) long, but it has many sheltered bays.

Besides the Mississippi River, there are several other important waterways in the state. They include the Pearl, Big Black, Tallahatchie, Yalobusha, Pascagoula, Tombigbee, and Yazoo Rivers. The Pascagoula River is nicknamed the "Singing River" because of the mysterious, unexplained humming noise that sometimes rises from the water.

The coastline of Mississippi is less than 50 miles (80 km) long, but there are many sheltered bays. Barrier islands separate Mississippi Sound from the deeper waters of the Gulf of Mexico.

GEOGRAPHY

CLIMATE AND
WEATHER

L ike other states in the Deep South, Mississippi has a subtropical climate. Summers are hot and humid. The average July high temperature is 91°F (33°C). On July 29, 1930, the thermometer rose to a steaming 115°F (46°C) in the town of Holly Springs. In the winter, temperatures usually rise to the mid-50s°F (13°C). The lowest temperature ever recorded in Mississippi happened on January 30, 1966, in the northeastern town of Corinth. That day, the mercury sank to -19°F (-28°C). Northern Mississippi gets small amounts of snow in winter, but it doesn't last long.

Athletes drink water to combat the heat during high school football practice in Jackson, Mississippi. With a subtropical climate, heat waves happen on a regular basis in the state.

Because of its location near the warm waters of the Gulf of Mexico, Mississippi gets a lot of rain. On average, the state receives 58 inches (147 cm) of precipitation. Thunderstorms are common. They often cause flooding. Spring floods can also be destructive.

Mississippi averages 32 tornadoes each year. Hurricanes don't often strike, but when these large, violent weather systems slam into the state, they can cause terrible damage. When Hurricane Katrina struck Mississippi in 2005, it caused much destruction and killed 238 people.

A professional storm chaser clings to a sign during the landfall of Hurricane Katrina in Gulfport, Mississippi, on August 29, 2005.

PLANTS AND ANIMALS

Forests occupy about 65 percent of Mississippi's land area. That is more than 19.5 million acres (7.9 million ha), which is a surprise to people who think Mississippi is mostly flat farmland. Mississippi has six national forests.

Common trees found growing in the state include spruce pine, loblolly pine, longleaf pine, bald cypress, white oak, live oak, cottonwood, maple, elm, hickory, pecan, sweetgum, and tupelo. Pines are more common in the south, while live oaks (some draped with Spanish moss) are more often found in marshy coastal areas.

The Pascagoula River flows past tree-lined shores.

Coreopsis or Tickseed

Magnolia

Gulf Fritillary Butterfly

One of the best-known trees in the state is the magnolia. They have lustrous green leaves. White flowers grow on the ends of the tree branches. The flowers bloom in late spring and have a sweet fragrance. Because they are so beautiful, Mississippi chose the magnolia for both its official state tree and flower.

Mississippi's official state wildflower is the coreopsis, also called tickseed. These daisy-like flowers are usually yellow. Many people plant them in gardens to attract butterflies.

Other wildflowers found in Mississippi include bur marigold, cardinal flower, lyre-leaf sage, partridge pea, bur marigold, black-eyed Susan, swamp rose mallow, and purple coneflower.

Mississippi has two official state land mammals. The first is the white-tailed deer. They are plentiful in the state's woodlands. Their name comes from the white color of the underside of their tails. The second state animal of Mississippi is the red fox. These members of the *canidae* family (which includes wolves and dogs) are omnivores. That means they eat small mammals and birds, as well as plants and insects.

Other animals found in Mississippi include rabbits, squirrels, black bears, opossums, coyotes, armadillos, weasels, raccoons, striped skunks, mice, and bats. The marshes of the coastal region hold many frogs, salamanders, and snakes. Venomous snakes can be dangerous if disturbed, but they are important because they prey on rodent pests. They include copperheads, cottonmouths, rattlesnakes, and eastern coral snakes. The official state reptile is the American alligator.

Mississippi's official state reptile is the American alligator.

Mississippi's state bird is the mockingbird. These medium-sized, gray-and-white birds can sing up to 200 songs, including those of other birds or even insects. Also commonly found in the skies of Mississippi are chickadees, goldfinches, cardinals, blue jays, wild turkeys, downy woodpeckers, robins, mourning doves, sandhill cranes, brown pelicans, and ospreys.

Mississippi's lakes and streams are full of catfish, bass, gar, perch, and trout. Saltwater creatures found in Mississippi's coastal waters include shad, black sea bass, Atlantic sturgeon, flounder, blue crab, and shrimp. The bottlenose dolphin is the official state marine mammal. The state fish is the largemouth bass.

Mockingbird

Bottlenose Dolphin

HISTORY

EMERALD MOUND

Mississippi's 8-acre (3-ha) Emerald Mound is the second largest temple mound in the United States. It was built and used from 1300-1600 AD by ancestors of the Natchez.

The ancestors of today's Native Americans arrived in the Mississippi region about 12,000 years ago. These Paleo-Indians eventually built settlements and grew crops. They also built large earthen mounds for religious purposes, such as burials.

In time, several Native American groups developed. The most powerful were the Choctaw, Chickasaw, Natchez, Biloxi, and Yazoo tribes.

In 1540, Spanish explorer Hernando de Soto passed through northeastern Mississippi with an army of several hundred conquistadors. They were searching for rumored gold, but found no treasure.

In the 1680s, France claimed much of the central part of North America, including Mississippi. The first French settlement was Fort Maurepas. It was built in 1699 on the Gulf Coast, near today's city of Biloxi. In 1716, the French founded the city of Natchez on the shores of the Mississippi River.

In 1763, Great Britain won the French and Indian War (1754-1763). The British took control of French territory, including Mississippi. However, after Great Britain lost the American Revolutionary War (1775-1783), it gave the territory to the young United States. Spain held part of Mississippi for a few years, but by 1798, Mississippi Territory became an official part of the United States.

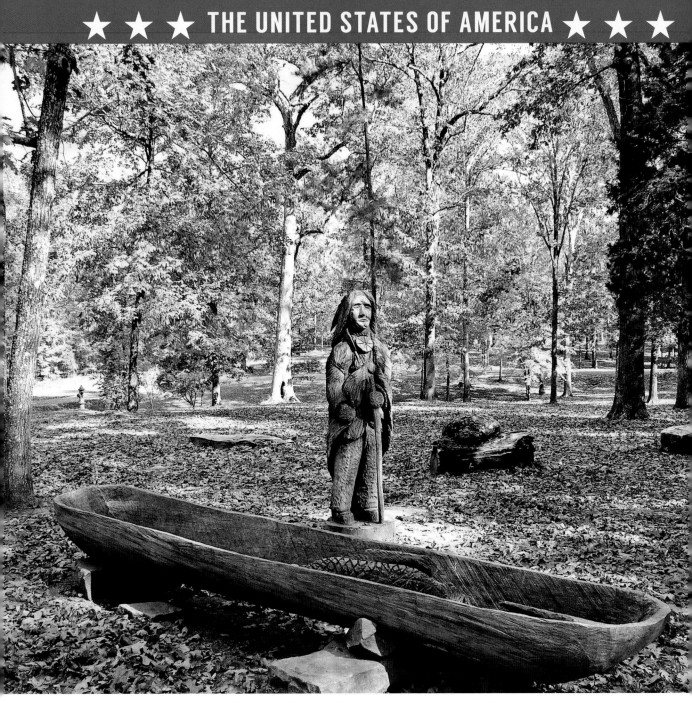

A carving of Chickasaw Chief Tishomingo (c. 1734-1838) stands in Tishomingo State Park in northeastern Mississippi. Tishomingo fought in the American Revolution and received a silver medallion from President George Washington. In 1838, he was forced to move west to Oklahoma, which was called Indian Territory. Chief Tishomingo died of smallpox during the trip.

HISTORY

In 1817, Mississippi Territory was split in half. The eastern half was named Alabama Territory. The western half became the state of Mississippi on December 10, 1817. It was the 20th state admitted to the Union. David Holmes became the state's first governor.

At the time of statehood, almost two-thirds of Mississippi was occupied by Native American tribes, especially the Choctaw and Chickasaw. In the 1820s and 1830s, the American government pressured the Native Americans to leave their native homes. They were forced to move west to Oklahoma, which was then called Indian Territory.

After the Native Americans left, cotton farmers took over their land. African slaves worked on the farms and picked the cotton. Slave labor and Mississippi's fertile soil made many farmers and plantation owners rich. The state became the nation's leading producer of cotton.

By 1860, African slaves made up more than half of Mississippi's population. Mississippi could not support its rich economy without fighting to keep slavery.

Slaves pick cotton on a Mississippi plantation in the 1800s.

During the Civil War, Union and Confederate forces clashed at Vicksburg, Mississippi, on May 19, 1863. Hard fighting continued for two more months before Vicksburg was captured by the Union army.

In 1861, Mississippi joined 10 other Southern states and formed their own country, called the Confederate States of America. During the Civil War (1861-1865), more than 80,000 Mississippians fought to keep their way of life. Northern states battled to abolish slavery and to keep the Union together.

One of the Civil War's most important battles was fought at Vicksburg, Mississippi. The Confederates were defeated. They lost control of the Mississippi River, which was vital for moving people and war supplies. By 1865, the Confederacy was forced to surrender.

After the Civil War, Mississippi's slaves were set free. Tens of thousands of Mississippians had lost their lives. The state's economy was shattered. Rebuilding the state was a long and difficult task. Cotton was no longer as profitable to grow, and there was little industry in the state. Before the Civil War, Mississippi was one of the wealthiest states. After the war, it became one of the poorest. Today, Mississippi continues to struggle financially, especially in rural areas.

After the slaves were set free, they were treated badly by former slave owners and their descendants. Some African Americans were able to buy small farms, especially in the Mississippi Delta region, but most remained poor. In the late 1800s and early 1900s, Mississippi River flooding and insect pests (especially boll weevils) destroyed crops and further hurt the economy.

People and their rescued belongings and animals surround the railroad station in flooded Egremont, Mississippi, during the Great Flood of 1927.

The March Against Fear brought hundreds of civil rights marchers together to walk 220 miles (354 km) from Memphis, Tennessee, to Jackson, Mississippi, in June 1966. The civil rights movement brought greater equality to all citizens.

Seeking better lives in northern and western cities, African Americans left Mississippi by the tens of thousands starting in the late 1800s. Another migration out of the state occurred in the 1940s and 1950s. Racial hatreds continued to boil for almost 100 years, until the United States passed new laws. The civil rights movement of the 1960s brought greater equality to all citizens.

In recent years, Mississippi has shifted away from depending so much on farming. Today, there are more jobs to be found in manufacturing and service industries. The state's cities are growing, and so are incomes. Most Mississippians today have put their bitter past behind them and are looking toward a brighter future.

DID YOU KNOW?

• The idea for the teddy bear came from an event that happened in Mississippi. In 1902, President Theodore Roosevelt traveled to the state on a bear-hunting expedition. The president had no luck hunting that day. Some of the other hunters captured a bear and tied it to a tree. The president refused to shoot it, saying it was unfair. The *Washington Post* newspaper later poked fun at the incident. It published a cartoon of Roosevelt next to a tiny bear. A toymaker named Morris Michtom from New York City, New York, saw the cartoon. It inspired him to create a cute stuffed toy bear. After receiving permission from the White House, he named his invention the Teddy Bear, after the president's nickname.

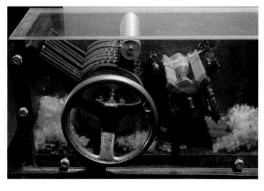

• The cotton gin was a machine invented by Eli Whitney in 1793. It used hooks and a wire screen to separate cotton fibers from the seeds. Before the cotton gin, the process had to be done by hand, and took much time and effort.

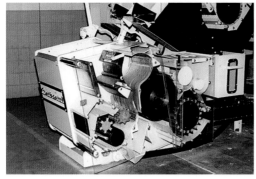

Cotton gins made the cotton industry more profitable. Tragically, it also led to more slavery in the South. Today, modern high-speed machines use powered cylinders and saws to process cotton.

Robert Johnson

• The blues is a kind of music invented by African Americans in the Deep South. It combines folk and spiritual music from Africa and Europe. Singing African folk music was a way for slaves to express their sorrows and hopes. The Delta blues is one of the earliest styles. It came from musicians in the Mississippi Delta region. It is known for using slide guitars and harmonicas. It is a very soulful kind of music, with flashes of fiery passion. It was first recorded in the 1920s. Some of the most famous Delta blues musicians include Robert Johnson, Muddy Waters, Big Joe Williams, and John Lee Hooker.

• Belzoni, Mississippi, is nicknamed the "Catfish Capital of the World." It is in the Mississippi Delta region, in Humphreys County. The county produces more farm-raised catfish than any other county in the United States. About 40,000 acres (16,187 ha) are underwater. They are used to farm catfish. Belzoni also hosts the annual World Catfish Festival every April. The festival features blues and country music, arts and crafts, and a catfish eating contest.

DID YOU KNOW?

PEOPLE

Elvis Presley (1935-1977) was one of the most popular musicians in the world during the 1950s and 1960s. Nicknamed "The King," he helped make rock and roll music popular. He played guitar and had a powerful, soulful singing voice. Presley combined country music with rhythm and blues. His concert performances had an energy that drove young fans wild. His first hit was "Heartbreak Hotel," which came out in 1956. He followed it

with dozens of smash songs, including "Hound Dog," "All Shook Up," "Jailhouse Rock," and "Love Me Tender." He has been inducted into five music halls of fame. Presley also had a successful acting career, starring in films that included *Jailhouse Rock*, *Blue Hawaii*, and *Viva Las Vegas*. Elvis Presley was born and spent his early childhood in Tupelo, Mississippi.

Brett Favre (1969-) is a former National Football League quarterback. Over a 20-year career, he set many NFL passing records. He is most remembered for his years with the Green Bay Packers, in which he led the team to a Super Bowl victory in 1997. Favre was born in Gulfport, Mississippi. He played football for four years for the University of Southern Mississippi in Hattiesburg.

James Earl Jones (1931-) is an Academy Award-winning actor. Over a 60-year career, he has won awards for his work on both stage and screen. His most popular roles were in films such as *The Great White Hope*, *Field of Dreams*, and *The Hunt for Red October*. He is also the voice of Darth Vader from *Star Wars*, and Mufasa from *The Lion King*. Jones was born in Arkabutla, Mississippi.

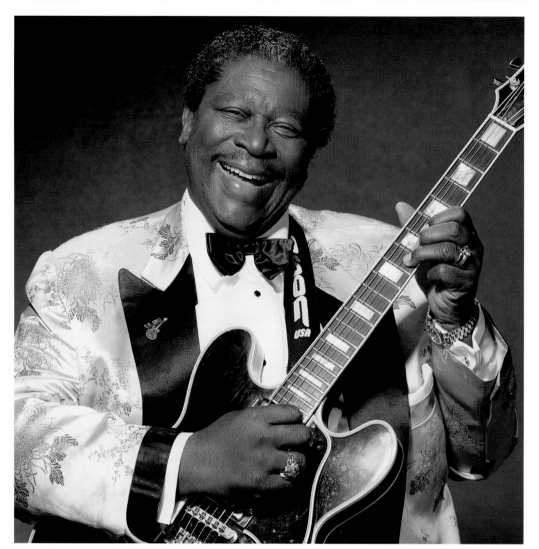

B.B. King (1925-2015) was one of the most influential blues musicians of all time. He was a singer, songwriter, and guitarist. Nicknamed "The King of the Blues," he taught himself to play guitar while growing up in the Mississippi Delta region. He sold many smash records over a career that lasted more than six decades. He continued to perform up to 200 concerts per year, even into his 70s. Some of his most popular hit songs included "The Thrill is Gone," "Rock Me Baby," and "Three O'Clock Blues." In 1987, he was inducted into the Rock and Roll Hall of Fame. B.B. King was born in Berclair, Mississippi.

William Faulkner (1897-1962) was an acclaimed, best-selling author who wrote many books about people and life in Mississippi. Many of his stories take place in fictional Yoknapatawpha County, which resembles the place where he lived. Faulkner's works are classics of American literature. His most popular books included *The Sound and the Fury*, *As I Lay Dying*, and *Light in August*. He also wrote many short stories, plays, and poetry. In 1949, he won the Noble Prize in Literature. Faulkner was born in New Albany, Mississippi.

CITIES

Jackson is the capital of Mississippi. It is also the state's largest city. Its population is 171,155. Together with its suburbs, about 540,000 people call the Jackson area home. It is located in southwestern Mississippi, along the shores of the Pearl River. It began in the early 1800s as a trading village called LeFleur's Bluff. In 1822, the city was renamed in honor of President Andrew Jackson. Today, the biggest employers include companies that make fabricated metal, machinery, electronics, and processed foods. Nicknamed the "City with Soul," Jackson is famous for blues music and Southern cooking. The Jackson Zoo opened in 1919. It contains 125 species of animals, including endangered white rhinos, leopards, orangutans, and Sumatran tigers.

Gulfport is the second-largest city in Mississippi. Its population is 71,750. It is located in southern Mississippi, along the coast of the Gulf of Mexico. Founded in 1898, the city has a deepwater port where large, oceangoing ships can dock. Gulfport attracts thousands of tourists with its many miles of white sandy beaches. There are also historical neighborhoods. Top employers include United States military bases, shipyards, health care, education, and casinos. In 2005, Gulfport was devastated by Hurricane Katrina. The city has worked hard to repair the damage.

Biloxi is the fifth-biggest city in Mississippi. Its population is 44,984. Like the city of Gulfport just to the west, Biloxi is located on the coast of the Gulf of Mexico in southern Mississippi. It was first settled in 1699, a few miles to the east in what is today the city of Ocean Springs. In 1838, the city was incorporated in its present location. Many people come to Biloxi to vacation. The city is nicknamed the "Seafood Capital of the World." It also has miles of white, sandy beaches and many casinos and resorts. The white Biloxi Lighthouse is a well-known landmark. It survived the winds and storm surges of Hurricane Katrina in 2005. The rest of the city was battered, but is quickly rebuilding.

Meridian is located in east-central Mississippi, near the Alabama border. Its population is 40,196. Founded in 1860, it began as a manufacturing and railroad transportation center. Today, it relies on health care, manufacturing, and the military. Meridian has a thriving arts community. There are many galleries and theaters in the city. Meridian is also famous for the historical architecture of its homes and downtown buildings.

Greenville is in northwestern Mississippi along the Arkansas border. Its population is 32,704. It is on the east bank of Lake Ferguson, an oxbow lake that was created when the Mississippi River changed course many years ago. Early Delta blues musicians played in city clubs in the 1940s and 1950s. In nearby Winterville State Park, visitors can see the remains of ancient earthen mounds built by Paleo-Indians.

TRANSPORTATION

Mississippi has 75,116 miles (120,887 km) of public roadways. Nine interstate highways whisk people and trucks loaded with goods across Mississippi and to other states. The main north-south interstate is I-55, which passes through the capital of Jackson. I-20 is a major east-west interstate. It also passes through Jackson. Trucks use Mississippi's network of state highways to haul crops from farming communities to markets in bigger cities.

The Mississippi River is the longest and busiest inland waterway in the United States. Mississippi has six ports along the river system. They include the cities of Rosedale, Greenville, and Vicksburg, plus Yazoo County, Claiborne County, and Natchez-Adams County. Mississippi's two biggest seaports are along the Gulf of Mexico. They are at Gulfport and Pascagoula. The Port of Pascagoula handles more than 33 million tons (29.9 million metric tons) of cargo annually.

The Port of Pascagoula is a major seaport on the Gulf of Mexico.

The Mississippi River runs past Natchez, Mississippi.

Mississippi has 27 railroad companies hauling freight on 2,452 miles (3,946 km) of track that crisscross the state. The most common products hauled by rail include chemicals, metal goods, paper, and refined petroleum. Amtrak's Crescent and City of New Orleans train lines carry passengers across the state.

Mississippi has 229 airports. Most are small. The two busiest are Gulfport-Biloxi International and Jackson-Evers International Airports.

The Amtrak Crescent crosses the Pearl River near Picayune, Mississippi.

NATURAL
RESOURCES

There are 10.9 million acres (4.4 million ha) of farmland in Mississippi. About 37,100 farms grow crops in the state's rich soil. In the past, cotton was the most valuable crop. Today, farmers make more money growing soybeans and corn, although cotton is still very important. Other crops grown in Mississippi include rice, hay, sweet potatoes, wheat, peanuts, blueberries, melons, and pecans. Top livestock products include beef and dairy cattle, hogs, and broiler chickens.

Mississippi has a lot of level bottomlands that can be flooded and used for aquaculture. Most fish farms are in the Mississippi Delta region. Thanks to foreign competition from Asia, catfish farming has dwindled in the United States. However, Mississippi still leads the nation in raising the tasty fish, which are found on menus in restaurants all over the South.

Workers harvest channel catfish from a fish farm pond in Itta Bena, Mississippi. The state leads the nation in raising catfish.

Cotton, once nicknamed "white gold," is harvested at a farm near Greenwood, in northwestern Mississippi. Greenwood has the second-largest cotton exchange in the United States.

Mississippi forests grow on approximately 65 percent of the state's land area. Many of those 19.5 million acres (7.9 million ha) are suitable for logging. The most active logging areas are in the southeastern part of the state.

Mining in Mississippi unearths bentonite, crushed stone, clay, fuller's earth, plus sand and gravel. The state produces a small amount of oil, natural gas, and coal. Most of these energy resources are located in the southern and central parts of the state.

NATURAL RESOURCES

INDUSTRY

Mississippi was once an agricultural powerhouse, thanks to its many cotton farms. Today, manufacturing and service industries produce the most jobs. Mississippi factories make transportation equipment, automobiles, ship parts, wood products, processed food, aerospace equipment, fabricated metals, and chemicals. Toyota automobiles are made in Blue Springs, near Tupelo, in a manufacturing plant the size of 45 football fields. Another large car-making factory is in Canton, Mississippi. It produces Nissan automobiles.

The city of Pascagoula, along the coast of the Gulf of Mexico, is home to Ingalls Shipbuilding. It is the largest manufacturing employer in Mississippi. About 12,000 workers build and repair large, oceangoing ships. Most are for the United States military, including modern Aegis guided missile destroyers.

More than 500,000 Toyota Corollas have been built in Blue Springs, Mississippi.

Stennis Space Center

The Space Launch System (SLS) RS-25 rocket engine is tested at NASA's Stennis Space Center near Bay St. Louis, Mississippi. The SLS will launch astronauts on missions to deep space and eventually to Mars.

NASA's John C. Stennis Space Center is located in southwestern Mississippi. It is the nation's largest facility for testing rocket engines. It tested the Saturn V rockets used on the Apollo moon missions. Today, the space center tests rockets used on vehicles such as the Orion spacecraft.

Tourism is a growing industry in Mississippi. Casino gambling was legalized in 1990. Since then, many large casinos and resorts have sprung up on coastal communities such as Gulfport and Biloxi.

INDUSTRY

SPORTS

Mississippi has no major league sports teams. However, it has several very popular minor league teams. The Biloxi Shuckers are a Minor League Baseball team. They are affiliated with the Milwaukee Brewers. They won a Southern League division title in 2015. The Mississippi Braves are a Minor League Baseball team from the city of Pearl. They are an affiliate of the Atlanta Braves. In 2008, they won a Southern League championship title.

The Mississippi RiverKings play ice hockey in the Southern Professional Hockey League. They play in Southaven, Mississippi. The Mississippi Brilla is a soccer team from the city of Clinton. They play in the Premier Development League's Southern Conference. They reached the Southern Conference finals in 2011.

*Ole Miss
Rebel Black Bear*

*Mississippi State
Bully the Bulldog*

*Southern Mississippi
Seymour the Golden Eagle*

College sports are big in Mississippi, especially football. The Ole Miss Rebels represent the University of Mississippi, in the city of Oxford. The university's football program started in 1890. Today, it has millions of loyal fans. Other popular college teams include the Mississippi State University Bulldogs and the University of Southern Mississippi Golden Eagles.

For outdoor lovers, there are many sports to pursue in Mississippi. Popular activities include hunting, fishing, swimming, boating, camping, hiking, bicycling, and much more.

ENTERTAINMENT

Mississippi is called the "Home of the Blues." The Delta Blues Museum is in Clarksdale, in the northwestern Mississippi Delta region. It is in a restored freight train depot built in 1918. Inside, there are exhibits, music education, and hundreds of musical instruments, recordings, photographs, and other items that tell the story of the blues. It even includes the cabin of legendary blues artist Muddy Waters.

A Mississippi Blues Trail Marker honors musician Hubert Sumlin.

MISSISSIPPI
EST. 2003
BLUES
COMMISSION

HUBERT SUMLIN

...ert Sumlin's sizzling guitar playing
...ed many of the classic Chicago blues
... Howlin' Wolf in the 1950s and '60s.
...putation in blues and rock circles
... him to ...lebrated career on his own
...olf's death ...976. In 2003 *Rolling Stone*
...christen... ... one of "The 100 Greatest
... of A... ...e." Sumlin was born on
...ntat... ...n a house that stood just
...th... ...on November 16, 1931.

Starting in 2006, music scholars and historians began putting up signs all over the state, marking where important events in blues history occurred. Today, the Mississippi Blues Trail has more than 170 markers where music lovers can learn about the music that has its roots in the state.

Mississippi is home to several symphony orchestras and dance troupes. The Mississippi Symphony Orchestra in Jackson performs more than 120 concerts statewide each year. The USA International Ballet Competition is held every four years in Jackson. Dancers from all over the world compete for Olympic-style medals and a chance at a professional career.

Mississippi has been the home state of some of the world's most celebrated authors, including William Faulkner, Tennessee Williams, John Grisham, Alice Walker, and Eudora Welty. Their books join millions of others in the state's many public libraries.

TIMELINE

10,000 BC—First Paleo-Indians arrive in Mississippi. After thousands of years, they group into Native American tribes.

1540—Hernando de Soto of Spain travels through Mississippi.

1699—France establishes the first European settlement in Mississippi, near today's city of Biloxi.

1716—French settlers found the city of Natchez on the shores of the Mississippi River.

1798—Spain gives up control of Mississippi to the United States. Mississippi becomes a United States territory.

1817—Mississippi becomes the 20th state admitted to the Union.

1820s—Native Americans are forced to leave the state. White farmers take over the former Indian lands. Cotton becomes an important crop. Slavery spreads.

1861—Mississippi breaks away from the United States and joins the Confederate States of America in order to keep slavery legal. The Civil War begins.

1865—The Confederacy is defeated. Slaves are freed.

Late-1800s & Mid-1900s—Many African Americans flee Mississippi to escape hardships.

1960s—The United States Congress and courts pass laws to stop unfair treatment of African Americans. Mississippi begins to modernize.

2005—Hurricane Katrina brings death and destruction to Mississippi coastal towns.

2008—The Mississippi Braves minor league baseball team wins the Southern League championship title.

2015—In its first season in the state, the Biloxi Shuckers minor league baseball team wins a Southern League division title.

INDEX

31901064596408